I KNOW MY FATHER

Neville Goddard

C L A S S Y
PUBLISHING

I KNOW MY FATHER
by Neville Goddard

Published by Classy Publishing, 2023

www.classypublishing.com
info@classypublishing.com

ISBN: 978-93-5522-325-8

Typeset in Minion Pro
Cover Design by Classy Publishing

CONTENTS

I

I AM

"My Father is he whom men call God, but I know my Father and men know not their God." My Father and Your Father are One. "Hear, O Israel, the Lord our God is One Lord." "I and my Father are One."

One Father made us all to live, move and have our being in Him the One. Who then is this ONE that we have in common? The one and only thing all men have in common is this, all men know that they are. This claim that we are, this awareness, is our Father.

There is no place that man can go and not know that he is. "If I take the wings of the morning and fly to the uttermost parts of the earth thou art there", I know that I Am.

"If I make my bed in Hell"- I know that I AM. If I should suffer from amnesia and completely forget my human identity I will still know that I AM. It is impossible for man to know that he is not. You can say I AM not that, but you cannot say I AM not, for your very knowing is a declaration that you are.

So whether you claim yourself to be or not to be, you are actually claiming that you are. Thus man is ever saying I AM. This knowing that we are, this awareness, is God the Father. The moment this unconditioned awareness becomes conditioned by claiming itself to be this that or the other, a differentiation takes place within this formless awareness, and our impersonal Father (Our real self) becomes personified as that which we have conceived ourselves to be.

This impersonal presence that we are may be likened to space, for space though formless gives form to all. If the formless space was extracted from the book you are reading, the body you wear, the earth you stand on, all would vanish.

Consciousness though formless, gives form to that which it is conscious of being, but the moment you withdraw your formless reality or consciousness from your conception of yourself (the form you wear) this conception passes away. A conception remains a formed reality only as long as the invisible reality wears it.

"My Father is Spirit (Formless) and they that worship him must worship him in Spirit and in

Truth." "I and my Father are one." My awareness of being is the formless Father who gives form to that which I am aware of being, and in so doing loses its formless, nameless presence, in the form and nature of its conception of itself.

As water loses its identity when mixed with things and yet remains untarnished when it is extracted through distillation, so the awareness the no-thing-loses itself in things-conceptions of itself and remains its immaculate self through spiritual distillation. You are spiritually distilled or extracted from your conception of yourself when you cease to be identified with it.

Now that you have found this one to be your Father, the Eternal Now, I AM, do not return to the prodigal state to beg for the crumbs of life. Remember your Father, the NOW, the only reality.

Claim yourself now, this moment, to be that which you desire to be and regardless of what your claim may be your Father, the awareness that is Now, will give it to you by becoming the thing claimed but you must ask him in this manner.

Be aware of being that for which you ask. No longer look for your Father in time and space, For your Father is the awareness that is now. "I and my Father are one, but my Father is greater than I." My awareness and that which I AM Aware of being are one, but I AM greater than that which I AM aware of being. The conceiver will ever be greater than his conception. The Father (Consciousness) is greater than his SON (conception of himself).

Now your eyes are opened. Your Father, God Almighty, has been revealed to you as your awareness of being.

II

I COME WITH A SWORD

Before you can enter into that peace which passeth all understanding, you must first be slain of all the illusions that now enslave you, the illusions of divisions.

If you are identified with race, creed or color and hear that with which you are identified, criticised and condemned, you will be automatically hurt by such criticism. Every attachment is a bar in your self-created prison. Your only escape lies in non-attachment. You must leave all and follow me. In Christ there is neither Greek nor Jew bond nor free.

Your present attachments are rooted in you because of your present conception of yourself. Your conception of yourself is the measuring rod by which you measure the world.

All things are judged in relationship to your present conception of yourself. Every man's conception of himself is a vibrant note in the Cosmic Symphony, which note automatically determines the value of all notes in relationship to itself.

Change your conception of yourself. Revalue yourself and you will automatically change your world. Man has always played the losing game by attempting to change his world, while he himself remained with his present values or conceptions of himself.

Jesus discovered this law. So instead of changing men he changed himself. He said, "And now I sanctify myself, that they also might be sanctified through the truth." He found himself to be the truth of all that he saw his world to be.

Truth is the sword that slays all but itself, and I AM (your awareness) is the truth. Therefore to be identified with anything other than being is to be enslaved, or limited by that with which you are identified.

You eternally objectify that which you are conscious of being, so you forever move in a world that is the perfect personification of that which you know yourself to be.

"To the pure all things are pure." This is a great hurdle to those who are constantly condemning the world. "There is therefore no condemnation to those in Christ Jesus."

It is recorded that the crowds left Jesus when he revealed the working of the law in these words, "No man cometh unto me save the Father in me draw him." And- "I and my Father are one."

They could not believe that they were the cause of all they saw their world to be. After thousands of years it is still the great stumbling block to all who see the world as something to be changed on the outside.

You and your conception of yourself are one. Your conception of yourself is the image you have made of your Father. This image fashions your world in your likeness, be it good bad or indifferent. Your Father is your awareness who limits you to that which you are aware of being. If you would change your world do so in truth, by knowing yourself to be all you see the world to be. You are not what you are because of anything in the world, on the contrary, The world is what it is because of what you are; the WHAT being the measure or value you have placed upon yourself. In short, your conception of yourself is the mould the conceiver (your true Self) uses to people your world. Begin to transform the world by claiming yourself to be that which you desire to see expressed in the world. Follow the example of Jesus who made Himself one with God, and found it not strange or robbery to do the work of God.

Freedom is not won by the sweat of the brow. Stop wrestling with the world, it is only a reflector. Jacob was freed only as he loosed that with which he wrestled. Likewise, you will be free only as you follow his example and loose your problem by not identifying yourself with it. For that which is bound in heaven (Consciousness) is bound on earth and that which is loosed in Heaven is loosed on earth. "You shall know the truth and the truth shall set you free." "I AM the truth." So in reality to know yourself the conditioned, is to be free from that which in your blindness you believed yourself to be. Leave all and just be ME.

III

THE FOUNDATION STONE

"Seek ye the Kingdom of Heaven and all things will be added unto you." Find the cause of things and you have found the secret of creation. You have heard it said, that "In the beginning God created the heaven and the earth", that "all things were made by him; and without him was not anything made that was made." No one questions the truth of this statement, but what one does want to know is- "who is God and where is God located?" In answer to the who you are told, "I AM God, I AM the lord, I AM hath sent me (the man Moses) unto you." As to the location of God you are told, "The Kingdom of God is within you." These two answers identify God as your awareness of being and locates him where you are aware of being. To be conscious of being is to silently declare, "I AM." As you read this page you are aware of being. This awareness, this consciousness of being, is God the creator. Awareness is that formless deep in which all things live, move and have their being, and apart from which things have no reality. This is the secret of the statement, "Before Abraham was, I AM, before the world was, I AM and when all things shall cease to be, I AM."

Awareness of being precedes all conceptions of itself and remains its formless self when all of its conceptions cease to be. The creator must precede creation, as the conceiver precedes his conceptions. Creation begins and ends in the Creator. Consciousness is the secret of all manifestion. Every creation passes through three stages in its unfoldment, conception, crucifixion and resurrection. Ideas, desires, ambitions are all conceptions moving within the motionless being, I AM. Consciousness is Father and all conceptions of itself are children bearing witness of their Father. Therefore, "I and my Father are one, but my Father is greater than I"; the conceiver and the conception are one, but the conceiver is greater than its conception.

Awareness is unconditioned. To be aware of being something or someone is conditioning the unconditioned. That which is defined is less than the definer. Awareness of being is the Almighty God, the Everlasting Father, upon whose shoulders is the government of the world. Awareness sustains and directs all things that it is aware of being. Consciousness of being is the eternal womb impregnating itself through the medium of desire. To be conscious of an urge or desire is to have conceived. To believe, by feeling yourself (The Formless) to be the thing desired, is to be crucified upon the form of the thing felt. To continue in the belief, feeling that you are now the thing desired until all doubts cease and a deep conviction is born that it is so is to be resurrected or visibly lifted into expressing the nature of the thing felt.

At this very moment you are resurrecting or expressing that which you are conscious of being. "I AM the resurrection and the life." I AM now out-picturing in the world round about me, as a living reality, that which I am now aware that I AM- and I shall continue to do so until I change my conception of myself. So your answer in consciousness to the eternal question, WHO AM I, Will determine your world and its every expression. Begin now to realize that I AM is the Lord God Almighty and beside ME (your awareness) There is no other God. Not I, John Doe is God but I AM, the awareness of being, is God. John Doe is only its present limitation or conception of itself. I am the limitless expressing through the limited conception of myself. To change the expression change the conception of yourself but do so in truth, not in words. That is turn your attention completely away from your present limitation and place it upon the new conception, until the awareness, your true being, is lost in the belief or conviction that I AM that I AM.

This is the reclothing or rebirth of your formless, nameless self. Your true self is a self, who no man sees, and who sees not itself, but sees only its conception of itself. In the beginning, now this moment, the idea or desire is swimming around in your consciousness seeking embodiment. Before the desire can be realized or resurrected, it must first become a cross or fixed point upon which consciousness is nailed. Awareness is the only living reality, the only resurrecting power. So to give life to my desire, I must in consciousness become aware of being the thing desired. "Let there be a firmament in the midst of the waters." In the midst of the waters or formless awareness, let there be a firmness or conviction that I AM the thing desired. Continue to stand upon this conviction or cross, and in ways unknown to you as man, you will realize or resurrect your desire. Life or awareness has ways that man (the conception) Knows not of its ways are past finding out. Life's present conception of itself as man is a mask that it wears. Within this being that you think you are, is your nameless self I AM.

The foundation of all expression is consciousness and other foundations no man can lay. Try as man will he cannot find another cause of manifestation other than God his consciousness of being. Man thinks he has found the cause of disease in germs; the cause of war in conflicting political ideologies and greed. All such discoveries of man, catalogued as they are as the essence of wisdom, are foolishness in the eyes of God. There is only one power and this power is God (Consciousness). It kills, it makes alive, it wounds, it heals, it does all things good, bad or indifferent.

A prisoner must have a jailer, a slave a master. A nation that feels itself to be imprisoned will automatically create a dictator. You could no more rub out a tyrant by destroying him, than you can your reflection by destroying the mirror. The consciousness of a nation produces its leaders. That which is true of a nation is true of an individual, for nations are made up of individuals. Man moves in a world that is nothing more nor less than his consciousness objectified. Not knowing this, he wars against his reflections while he keeps alive the light and the images which throw the reflections. "I AM the light of the world." I AM (consciousness is the light.) That which I am conscious of being (my conception of myself) such as, I am rich, I am healthy, I am free-are the images.

The world is the mirror magnifying all that I AM conscious of being. Stop trying to change the world, it is only a mirror telling you who you are.

The man who is conscious of being free or imprisoned is expressing that which he is conscious of being. I do not care what men have diagnosed your problem to be. A problem might have a history ages long, yet I know it will vanish in the twinkle of an eye, if you will faithfully follow this instruction.

Ask yourself this simple question. How would I feel if I were free? The very moment you sincerely ask this question the answer comes.

No man can tell another how that other would feel if his desire were suddenly realized. But everyone would know how he himself would feel, for such feeling would be automatic.

The feeling or thrill that comes to one in response to his self-questioning is the Father state of consciousness or Foundation Stone, from which will come the thing felt. Just how this feeling will embody itself no one knows but it will for the Father (consciousness) has ways that no man knows of.

Make the new feeling natural by wearing it. All things express their nature, so you must wear this feeling until it becomes your nature. It might take a moment or a year it is entirely up to you. The moment all doubts vanish and you feel I AM this, you begin to bear the fruit of the nature of the thing you are feeling yourself to be. When a person buys a new hat or pair of shoes he thinks everyone knows that they are new. He feels unnatural with them on until he wears them long enough to make them natural. The same applies to the wearing of the new state of consciousness.

When you ask yourself the question, "How would I feel if my desire were this moment realized?" -the automatic reply is so new that you Feel that it is not yours, that it is not true. Therefore, you instantly put this new state of consciousness off and immediately return to your problem because it is more natural. Not knowing that consciousness is ever out-picturing itself in conditions round about you- You, like Lot's wife, look back upon your problem and once again become hypnotized by its naturalness. Do you not hear the words of Jesus (salvation)? "Leave all and follow me- let the dead bury their dead." Your problem might have you so hypnotized by its seeming reality and naturalness, that you find it difficult to wear the new feeling, or consciousness of your saviour but wear it you must if you would have results. The stone (Consciousness) which the builders rejected (would not wear) is the chief corner Stone and other foundations no man can lay.

IV

THE I'M-PRESSION

Every impression must become the affirmation of that which is to be. To say that I shall be great or that I shall be free is a confession that I am not great and I Am not free. To see yourself as becoming anything is to know that I am not that thing. To be Impressed- is to be I'm-pressed-first person, present tense. All expressions are the result of I'm-pressions. Only as I can claim myself to be that which I desire to be will I express such claims. Let all your desires be impressions of that which is, not that which is to be. For I'm (your awareness) is God, and God is the fullness of all, the Eternal NOW-I AM-I'm.

Signs follow, they do not precede. You will never see the signs of that which is. Take no thought of tomorrow, for your tomorrows are the expressions of your todays impressions. "Now is the accepted time. The Kingdom of Heaven is at hand." Jesus (salvation) said, "I am with you always." Your awareness is the savior that is with you always. But, if you deny him, he will deny you also. You deny him by claiming that he will appear, as millons today are doing when they claim that salvation is to come, which claim is the equivalent of saying, "We are not saved." You must stop looking for your savior to appear and claim yourself to be saved now, and the signs of your claims shall follow.

When the widow was asked, "what had she in her house," there was recognition of substance, Now, in her claim of three drops of oil, not empty measures. Three drops become a gusher if claimed. For your awareness magnifies all that it is conscious of being. To claim that I shall have oil (Joy) is to confess that I have empty measures, which consciousness of lack, will produce lack. God, your awareness, is no respecter of persons and can only express that with which it is impressed. Your every desire is determined by your need. Desires are automatic. Knowing that you are aware of the desire and that your awareness is God, You should look upon each desire as the spoken words of God, telling you of that which is. "Turn from the seeing of man whose breath is in his nostrils." For he sees his desire as that which is not. We shall ever be that which we are (aware)- so never again claim, I shall be that. Let all claims from now on be-"I AM that I AM."

"Before they ask I have answered." Before you have time to think, the solution of your problem was given you in the form of your desire. The blind, the lame, the halt, all automatically desire freedom from limitation. Man is so schooled in the belief that his desires are things to struggle over, that he in his ignorance, denies his savior who is constantly knocking at the door of consciousness (I AM the Door) to be let in. Would not your desire, if realized, save you from your problem? To let your savior in is the easiest thing in the world. Things must be, to be let in. You are conscious of a desire, therefore, the desire is something that you are aware of now. Your desire, though invisible, must be affirmed by you to be something that is real. "God calleth those things which be not (are not seen) as though they were." The claim I AM He (the thing desired) is letting your savior in.

Every desire is the savior's knock at the door. This knock, every man hears. Man opens the door for him to enter when he claims- I AM He. See to it that you let your savior in, by letting the thing desired press itself upon you, until you are I'mpressed with the Nowness of your savior, and utter the cry of Victory, "It is finished."

V

HE WHO HAS

"For he that hath, To him shall be given and To he that hath not, from him shall be taken even that which he hath." Though many look upon this statement to be the most cruel and unjust of the sayings attributed to Jesus- creating as it has the world over the many popular remarks, such as, the rich get richer and the poor get children; he who has gets, etc.,-it still remains a most just and merciful law based upon a changeless principle.

God is no respecter of persons. God, as we have discovered, is that unconditioned awareness who gives to each and all, that which they are aware of being. To be aware of being or having anything is to be or have that which you are aware of being. Upon this changeless principle all things rest. It is impossible for anything to be other than that which it is aware of being. "To him that hath (That which he is aware of Being) It shall be given"- good, bad or indifferent. It does not matter what it is that you are aware of being, you will receive pressed down, shaken together and running over, all that you are conscious of being. In keeping with this same changeless law, "To Him that hath not, It shall be taken from and added to the one that hath." So the rich do get richer and the poor get poorer. Yes, He who has Gets.

You cannot express that which you are not conscious of being. You cannot serve two masters. Your master is ever that state of consciousness with which you are identified. Therefore that which is not in consciousness is taken from it- (because it was never part of it) and added to that consciousness which it is aware of it. All things gravitate to that consciousness with which they are in tune, and likewise, all things disentangle themselves from that consciousness with which they are not in tune. So instead of joining the chorus of the have nots who insist on destroying those who have, recognize this changeless law of expression and consciously claim yourself to be that which you have decided to be. After your decision is made and your conscious claim established, continue in your confidence until you receive your reward. For as the day follows the night, you will receive that which you have consciously claimed for yourself.

Thus, that which to the sleeping orthodox world is a cruel and unjust law, becomes to the enlightened, the most merciful and just statement of truth. "I am come not to destroy but to fulfill."

Knowing that God does not destroy anything, see to it that you are that, claim yourself to be that which you want him to fill-full. Nothing is destroyed. All are fulfilled.

VI

CIRCUMCISION

Circumcision is the operation which removes the veil that hides the head of creation. The physical act has nothing to do with the spiritual act.

The whole world could be physically circumcised and yet remain unclean and blind leaders of the blind. The spiritually circumcised have had the veil of darkness removed and know themselves to be Christ, the light of the World.

Let me now perform the spiritual operation on you, the reader. This act is performed on the eighth day after birth; eight, because eight is the figure that has neither beginning nor ending. Furthermore, the ancients symbolized the eighth numeral as an enclosure or veil, within and behind which lay buried the mystery of creation. Thus, the secret of the operation on the eighth day is in keeping with the nature of the act, which act, is to reveal the eternal head of creation; that changeless something in which all things begin and end, and remains its eternal self when all things cease to be. This mysterious something is your awareness of being. At this moment you are aware of being, but you are aware of being someone. This someone is the veil that hides the being that you really are. You are first conscious of being, then you are conscious of being man. After the veil of man is placed upon your faceless self you become conscious of being a member of a certain race, nation, family, creed, etc. The veil to be lifted in spiritual circumcision is the veil of man, but before this can be done, you must cut away the adhesions of race, nation, family and so on.

"In Christ there is neither Greek nor Jew, bond nor free, male nor female." You must leave father, mother, brother and follow me. To accomplish this you must stop identifying yourself with these divisions, by becoming indifferent to such claims. Indifference is the knife that severs. Feeling is the tie that binds. When you can look upon man as one grand brotherhood without distinction of race, creed or color, then you will know that you have severed these adhesions. With these ties cut all that now separates you from your true being is your belief that you are man.

To remove this last veil, you must drop your conception of yourself as man, by knowing yourself just to be. Instead of the consciousness of -I AM Man, let there be just-I AM-Faceless, Formless Awareness. Then, unveiled and awake you will declare and know that-I AM is God and beside me, this awareness, there is no God. This mystery is told in the bible story of Jesus washing the feet of his disciples. It is recorded that Jesus laid aside his garments and took a towel and girded himself. Then after washing his disciples' feet he wiped them with the towel wherewith he was girded. Peter protested and was told that unless his feet where washed, he would have no part of Jesus. Peter replied, "Lord, not my feet only, but also my hands and head." Jesus answered and said, "He that is washed needeth not save to wash feet, but is clean every whit."

Common sense would tell the reader that a man is not clean all over just because his feet are washed. So he should either discard this story or look for its hidden meaning. Every story of the Bible is a psychological drama taking place in the consciousness of man and this is no exception.

This washing of the disciples' feet is the mystical story of spiritual circumcision or the revealing of the secrets of the lord.

Jesus is called the lord. You are told that the Lord's name is I AM-Je Suis. "I am the lord that is my name." - Isaiah 42:8. Jesus is girded with a towel, therefore his secrets are hidden. Jesus or Lord symbolizes your awareness of being, whose secrets are hidden by the towel- (consiousness of man). The foot symbolizes the understanding (Walk ye in his footsteps-understanding) which must be washed by the lord-awareness-of all human beliefs or conceptions of itself. As the towel is removed to dry the feet the secrets of the Lord are revealed.

In short, the removing of the belief that you are man reveals your awareness as the head of creation. Man is the foreskin hiding the head of creation. I AM the lord hidden by the veil of man.

VII

CRUCIFIXION AND RESURRECTION

The events of crucifixion and resurrection are so interwoven they must be explained together for one determines the other. This mystery is symbolized on earth in the rituals of Good Friday and Easter. You have observed that these days are not fixed but change from year to year. They fall anywhere from the last week of March to the last week of April. The day is determined in this manner. The first Sunday after the full moon in Aries is celebrated as Easter. Aries begins on the 21st day of March and marks the beginning of Spring. This movable date should tell the observant one to look for some interpretation, other than the one given him.

Seen from the earth, the Sun in its northern passage appears at the Spring season of the year to cross the imaginary lineman calls the equator. So it is said, by the mystic, to be crossified or crucified that man might live. They noticed that soon after this event took place, all nature began to rise or resurrect itself from its long winter's sleep, therefore they concluded that this disturbance of nature at this season of the year was due directly to this crossing. Thus they believed that the Son must have shed his blood at the passover. If these dates marked the death and resurrection of Jesus they would be fixed like all other historical events, but this is not the case. However these dates do symbolize the death and resurrection of the lord, but this lord is your awareness of being. It is recorded that he gave His life that you may live- "I AM come that you might have life and that you might have it more abundantly."

As Spring is the time of the year when the millons of seeds, which all winter lay buried in the ground, suddenly spring into visibility that man might live and because the mystical drama of the crucifixion and resurrection is in the nature of this yearly change, it is celebrated at this Spring season of the year but actually it is taking place every moment of time. The being that is crucified is our awareness of being. The cross is your conception of yourself. The resurrection is the lifting into visibility of this conception of yourself. Far from being a day of mourning Good Friday should be a day of rejoicing, for there can be no resurrection without a crucifixion. The thing to be resurrected in your case is that which you desire to be. To do this, you must feel yourself to be the thing desired. You must feel I AM that, for I AM the resurrection and the life. Yes, I AM (Your awareness of being) is the power resurrecting and making alive that which you are aware of being.

Two shall agree on touching anything and I shall establish it on earth. The two agreeing are You (your awareness) and the thing desired (that which you have decided on to be, through becoming aware of it). When this agreement is attained, the crucifixion is completed. Two have crossed or crossified each other. I AM and that (the thing desired) have joined. I AM now nailed upon the form of that.

The nail that binds you upon the cross is the nail of feeling. The mystical marriage is now consummated and the result will be the birth of a child or the resurrection of a son bearing witness of his Father.

Consciousness is wedded to that which it is conscious of being. The world of expression is the child confirming this union. The day you cease to be conscious of being that which you are now conscious of being, that day your child or expression shall die and return to the bosom of his father, the faceless, formless awareness. All expressions are the results of such mystical marriages. So the priests are correct when they say, all true marriages are made in Heaven and can only be dissolved in Heaven. But let me clarify this statement by telling you that Heaven is not a locality, it is a state of consciousness. The Kingdom of Heaven is within you. In Heaven (consciousness) God is touched by that which he is aware of being. "Who has touched Me? For I perceive virtue has gone out of me." The moment this touching (feeling) takes place, there is an off-springing or going-out-of-me into visibility, taking place.

The day man feels I AM free, I AM wealthy, I AM strong, God (I AM) is touched by these qualities or virtues, and the results of such touching will be seen in the birth or resurrection of the qualities felt. For man must have visible confirmation of all that he is conscious of being. Now you will know why man or manifestation is always made in the image of God.

Your awareness images and out-pictures all that you are aware of being. "I AM the Lord and beside Me there is no other God." I AM the resurrection and the Life!

VIII

NO OTHER GOD

"Thou shalt have no other God beside me." As long as man entertains the belief in powers apart from himself, so long will he rob himself of the being that he is. Every belief in powers apart from yourself, whether for good or evil, will become the moulds of the graven images you will worship.

The belief in the potency of drugs to heal, diets to strengthen, monies to secure, are the values or money changers that must be thrown out of the Temple. "Ye are the Temple of the living God"- a Temple made without hands.

It is written, "My house shall be called of all nations a house of prayer, but ye have made it a den of thieves."

Your beliefs in the potency of things are the thieves that rob you. There is only one power, one Savior-I AM He. It is your belief in the thing and not the thing itself that aids you. Therefore, stop transferring the power that you are to things round about you. Claim yourself to be the power which you have in your ignorance given to another.

It is easier for a camel, burdened as he is with the so-called treasures of life, to go through the needle's eye (a small gate in the walls of Jerusalem, so named because of its narrowness) than a rich man (the opinionated man filled with his human values) to enter the Kingdom of Heaven. Man is so filled with human values (riches) as to the reason of things, that he cannot, through so dark a veil as the wisdom of man, see that the only reason or value to anything is that all things are expressing perfectly that which they are conscious of being. When man realizes that the consciousness of a quality expresses that quality without the aid of anything else, he will become the poor man, the foolish man, who has no reason for anything happening other than that which is happening, is perfectly expressing that which it is conscious of being. Such a one has thrown out the money changers or many values and has now established one value: consciousness.

The Lord is in his holy temple. Consciousness dwells within that which it is conscious of being. I AM man-is the Lord and his Temple. Knowing that the consciousness of wealth produces wealth, as the consciousness of poverty produces poverty, He forgives all men for being what they are. For all are expressing (without the aid of another) that which they are conscious of being. He knows that a change of consciousness will produce a change of expression, so instead of sympathizing with the beggars of life at the temple gate, he declares, "Silver and gold have I none (for thee) but such as I have (the consciousness of freedom) give I unto thee." Stir up the gift within you. Stop begging, and claim yourself to be that which you were begging for. Do this and you too will jump from your crippled world into the world of freedom, singing praises to the lord, I AM. "Far greater is he that is in you, than he that is in the world." This cry of everyone who finds His awareness of being to be God.

Your recognition of this fact will automatically cleanse the temple of the thieves and robbers and restore to you that dominion over things which you lost the moment you forgot the command, "Thou shalt have no other God beside me!"

IX

THY WILL BE DONE

"Not my will, but thine be done." This resignation is not one of blind fatalism but it is the illumined realization that, "I can of myself do nothing, the Father within me he doeth the work." When man wills he attempts to make something appear in time and space which he knows does not now exist. He is not aware of what it is he is really doing. But, what he actually does is this. He consciously states, I do not possess the capacities to express it now, but I will acquire these capacities in time. In short-I AM not, but I will be.

Man does not realize that consciousness is the Father who does the work, so he attempts to express that which he is not conscious of being. Such struggles are doomed to disappointment, for only the present expresses itself. Unless I am conscious of being that which I seek, I will not find it. God (your awareness) is the substance and fullness of all. God's will is the recognition of that which is, not of that which shall be. Instead of seeing this saying as, "Thy, will be done"- see it as, "Thy will, be done" (is done). The works are finished. The principle by which all things are made visible is eternal. Even though, "Eyes have not seen nor ears heard, neither hath it entered into the hearts of man, the things which God hath prepared for those who love the law."

When a sculptor looks at a formless piece of marble he sees buried within its formless self, his finished piece of art. So the sculptor instead of making his masterpiece, merely reveals it, by removing that part of the marble which hides his conception.

The same applies to you. In your formless awareness- I AM-lies buried all that you will ever conceive yourself to be. The recognition of this truth will transform you from that of an unskilled laborer, who tries to make it so, to that of a great artist, who recognizes it to be so.

Your claim that you are now that which you want to be, will remove the veil of human darkness with its-I will be-and reveal your perfect claim-I AM that.

God's will was expressed in the words of the widow, "It is well." Man's will would have been, "It shall be well." To state I shall be well is to say, "I AM ill." God, the Eternal now, is not mocked by words or vain repetition. God continually personifies that which is.

Thus, the resignation of Jesus (who made himself Equal with God) was turning from the recognition of lack (which the future indicates with I shall be) to the recognition of supply by claiming- I AM that.

Now you will see the wisdom in the words of the prophet when he stated, "Let the weak say, I AM Strong." - Joel 3:10. Man in his blindness will not heed the prophet's advice, so, he continues to claim himself to be weak, poor wretched and all the other undesirable expressions from which he is trying to free himself, by ignorantly claiming that he will be free from them.

There is only one door through which That Which You Seek can enter your world. When you say, I AM, you are declaring yourself to be first person, present tense. Again, to know that I AM, is to be conscious of being consciousness is the only door. Therefore, unless you are conscious of being That Which You Seek, you seek in vain. If you judge after appearances you will continue to be enslaved by the evidence of your senses. To break from this hypnotic spell of the senses you are told, "go within and shut the door." The door of the senses must be tightly shut before your new claim can be honored. This closing the door of the senses is not as difficult as it at first appears to be. It is done without effort. It is impossible to serve two masters at the same time. The Masterman serves in that which he is conscious of being. I am Lord and Master of that which I am conscious of being.

It is no effort for me to conjure poverty if I AM conscious of being poor. My servant poverty is compelled to follow me (Consciousness of Poverty) as long as I AM (The Lord) conscious of being poor. Instead of fighting against the evidence of the senses, you simply claim yourself to be that which you desire to be. As your attention is placed on this claim, the door of the senses, automatically close against your former master- that which you were conscious of being. As you become lost in the feeling of being this which you are now claiming yourself to be true of yourself, the doors once more open (but as you have discovered, they permit only the present that which I AM now conscious of being-to enter) and you behold your world expressing that which you are conscious of being. Therefore let us follow the example of Jesus, who, realizing that he could as man do nothing to change his present picture of lack closed the door of his senses and went to his Father, to whom all things are possible. Having denied the evidence of his senses, he claimed himself to be that which but a moment before his senses told him that he was not. Knowing that consciousness expresses its likeness on earth, he remained in the claimed consciousness until the doors (his senses) opened and confirmed the Rulership of the Lord. Remember, I AM is Lord of all. Never again use the will of man which claims I will be. Be as resigned as Jesus, and claim- I AM that.

X

BE EARS THAT HEAR

"Let these sayings sink down in your ears, for the Son of Man shall be delivered into the hands of man." Be not as those who have eyes and see not, and ears and hear not. Let these l revelations sink deep into your ears. For after the son (idea) is made manifest, man with his false values (reason) will attempt to explain the why and wherefore of the son's expression, and in so doing will rend him to pieces. After men have agreed that a certain thing is impossible to do, let someone accomplish the impossible thing–and all, including the wise ones who said it could not be done– will begin to tell you why it happened. After they are all through tearing the seamless robe (cause of manifestation) apart, they will be as far from the truth as they were when they proclaimed it impossible.

As long as man looks for the cause of expression in places other than the expressor, he looks in vain.

For thousands of years man has been told, "I AM the life and light of the world." "No manifestation cometh unto me save I draw it."

But man will not believe it, he prefers to believe in causes outside of himself. The moment that which was not seen becomes seen, man is ready to explain the cause and purpose of its appearance. Thus the Son of Man (ideas of manifestation) is constantly being destroyed by the hands (reasonable explanation or wisdom) of man. Now that your awareness is revealed to you as cause of all expression, do not return to the darkness of Egypt with its many Gods. There is but one God. The one God is your awareness. "And all the inhabitants of the earth are reputed as nothing. And he doeth according to his will in the army of heaven, and among the inhabitants of the earth and none can stay his hand, or say unto him, what doest thou?" If the whole world should agree that a thing could not be done, and you became aware of being that which they had agreed upon could not be expressed–you would express it. Your awareness never asks permission to express that which you are aware of being. It does so naturally and without effort in spite of the wisdom of man and the opposition of the armies of both heaven and earth.

"Salute no man by the way", is not a command to be insolent or unfriendly, but a reminder not to recognize a superior, nor to see in anyone a barrier to your expression. For none can stay your hand or question your ability to express that which you are conscious of being. Do not judge after the appearances of a thing, for all are as nothing in the eyes of God. When the disciples, through their judgment of appearances, saw the insane child, they thought it a more difficult problem to solve than others they had seen–and so failed to achieve a cure. In judging after appearances they forgot that all things were possible to God. Hypnotized as they were to the reality of appearances they could not feel the naturalness of sanity. The only way for you to avoid such failures is to constantly bear in mind that your awareness is the Almighty, all-wise presence, who without help, effortlessly out-pictures that which you are aware of being. Be perfectly indifferent to the evidence of the senses, so that you may feel the naturalness of your desire–and your desire will be realized. Turn from appearances and feel the naturalness of perfect sanity and sanity will embody itself. Your desire is the solution of your problem. As the desire is realized, the problem is dissolved. Your desires are the invisible realities which respond only to the commands of God. God commands the invisible to appear by claiming himself to be the thing commanded. "He made himself equal with

God and found it not robbery to do the works of God." Now, "let this saying sink deep in your ear" – BE CONSCIOUS OF BEING THAT WHICH YOU WANT TO APPEAR.

Printed in the USA
CPSIA information can be obtained
at www.ICGtesting.com
LVHW041647301124
797921LV00003B/384